BIG BEASTLY BOOK OF BART SIMPSON

TITAN BOOKS

BIG BEASTLY BOOK OF BART SIMPSON

Copyright © 2004, 2005 & 2007 by
Bongo Entertainment, Inc. All rights reserved.
No part of this book may be used or reproduced in any manner whatsoever
without written permission except in the case of brief quotations
embodied in critical articles and reviews. For information address
Bongo Comics Group c/o Titan Books
P.O. Box 1963, Santa Monica, CA 90406-1963

Published in the UK by Titan Books, a division of Titan Publishing Group,
144 Southwark St., London SE1 0UP, under licence from Bongo Entertainment, Inc.

FIRST EDITION: MAY 2007

ISBN 1-84576-411-0
ISBN-13 978-1-84576-411-1

4 6 8 10 9 7 5 3

Publisher: MATT GROENING
Creative Director: BILL MORRISON
Managing Editor: TERRY DELEGEANE
Director of Operations: ROBERT ZAUGH
Art Director: NATHAN KANE
Art Director Special Projects: SERBAN CRISTESCU
Production Manager: CHRISTOPHER UNGAR
Legal Guardian: SUSAN A. GRODE
HarperCollins Editors: HOPE INNELLI, JEREMY CESAREC

Trade Paperback Concepts and Design: SERBAN CRISTESCU

Contributing Artists:
KAREN BATES, JOHN COSTANZA, SERBAN CRISTESCU, JOHN DELANEY,
LUIS ESCOBAR, NATHAN HAMILL, JASON HO, NATHAN KANE, JAMES LLOYD,
JEANETTE MORENO, BILL MORRISON, PHYLLIS NOVIN, PHIL ORTIZ, PATRICK OWSLEY,
ANDREW PEPOY, MIKE ROTE, HOWARD SHUM, ART VILLANUEVA, CHRIS UNGAR

Contributing Writers:
JAMES W. BATES, TONY DIGEROLAMO, TOM PEYER, ERIC ROGERS

PRINTED IN ITALY

TABLE OF CONTENTS

PG. 7   BATTER-UP BART

PG. 22   THE THREE STAGES OF TEACHING

PG. 25   CUFF IT UP!

PG. 36   FINAL DETENTION

PG. 46   BART BURGER

PG. 48   BAIT AND CACKLE

PG. 54   BIRTH OF A SALESMAN

PG. 63   BART VS. THE ONE-MAN SCHOOL

PG. 75   BART SIMPSON EXPLAINS "THE SICK DAY"

PG. 77   SPECIAL DELIVERY

PG. 80   KWIK-E-BART

PG. 83   GRAMPA BART

PG. 86   FLU SHOT

PG. 91   BART'S GOT SPIRIT!

PG. 101   NELSON MUNTZ'S GUIDE TO GROWN-UP NERDS

PG. 103   THE KISS OF BLECCH

PG. 106   MAGGIE & MOE: THE WILLFUL WILL

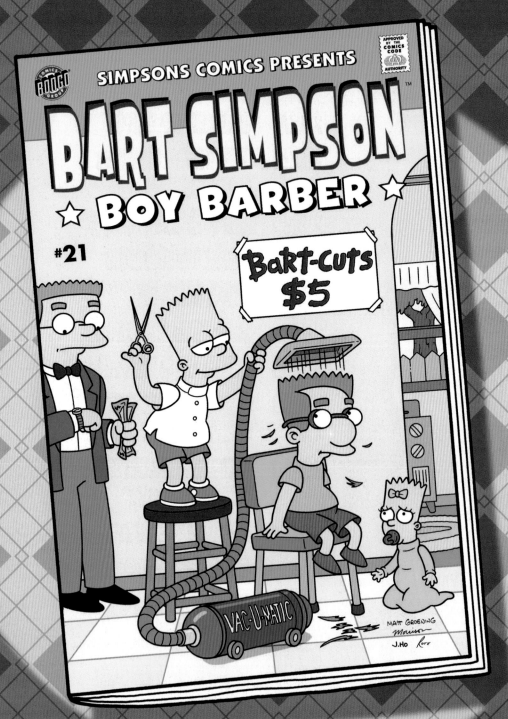

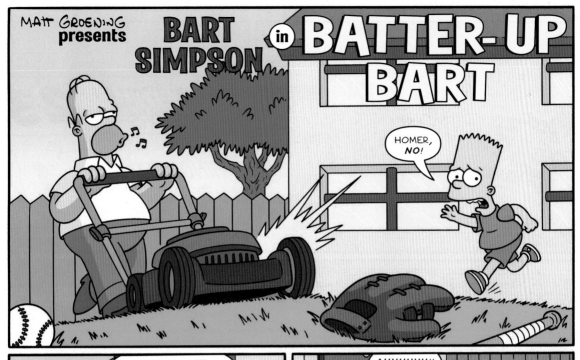

MATT GROENING presents BART SIMPSON in BATTER-UP BART

HOMER, *NO!*

YOU ALMOST RAN OVER MY LUCKY BASEBALL GLOVE.

RELAX. I'LL GET IT OUT OF THE WAY.

PUNT!

AHHHHHH!! MY LUCKY GLOVE!

SHRED!

WHOOPS. SORRY BOY.

DAD! I HAVE A GAME ON SATURDAY! YOU GOTTA BUY ME A NEW GLOVE!

SORRY, NO CAN DO. I SPENT MY WHOLE PAY CHECK RENTING THIS WOOD-CHIPPER.

WHAT FOR?

I WAS GETTING TIRED OF THOSE LITTLE JARS OF SALSA! THEY NEVER GIVE YOU ENOUGH.

SEE THAT? NOW THAT'S A *MAN-SIZED* QUANTITY FOR *MAN-SIZED* DIPPING!

SHRED! SHRED! SHRED!

GRINGO GRADE **MACHO'S NACHOS!**

MUY SUPER GRANDE SIZE!

HERE, HELP ME GET THIS BAG OPEN.

SANTO FUMA! LOS NACHOS SON ENORMES!

THAT SATURDAY...

| SHELBYVILLE RAPTORS | **23** |
| SPRINGFIELD LI'L TOPES | **1** |

NICE GAME, LOSERS!

HA HA HA HA!

THIS SUCKS!

WE TRIED OUR BEST, BART. TWENTY-THREE TO ONE ISN'T SO AWFUL. AT LEAST WE WEREN'T SHUT OUT.

WE LOST ONE *HUNDRED* AND TWENTY-THREE TO ONE! THE SCOREBOARD DOESN'T GO THAT HIGH!

I'M A GOALIE!

FACE IT, LIS, WE CAN'T COMPETE! OUR UNIFORMS WERE DONATED BY THE THRIFT SHOP, OUR BATS ARE MADE OF BALSA WOOD, AND WE DON'T EVEN HAVE A DECENT THIRD BASE!

13

I'M DOING THE BEST I CAN!

PERHAPS WE SHOULD MAKE A LIST OF GRIEVANCES AND TAKE IT UP WITH THE COACH.

AS YOUR LEAGUE COORDINATOR, I MUST TELL YOU YOUR TEAM IS IN DANGER OF BEING DISQUALIFIED.

LISTEN YE NOODLE-BRAINED PANSY! COACH WILLIE DINNA NEED THE LIKES OF YOU TELLIN' HIM HOW TO COACH!

YOU HAVE TO CUT THE OUT-FIELD ACCORDING TO *LEAGUE RULES*!

TA BLAZES WITH YER RULES! *WILLIE QUITS*!

I'M SORRY KIDS, IF YOU DON'T HAVE AN ADULT COACH, YOU CAN'T HAVE A TEAM.

I'M SURE MY DAD WOULD LOVE TO COACH US, SIR.

LISA, HOMER GETS WINDED JUST MARKING A BASE-BALL SCORECARD.

BUT WHO ELSE WILL BE WILLING TO TAKE THIS RAGTAG GROUP OF NERDLY MISFITS AND TURN US INTO A WINNING TEAM?

LISA! THAT'S *IT*! I KNOW A MAN WHOSE NAME IS *SYNONYMOUS* WITH "NERDLY MISFITS"!

GREETINGS, TEAM. YOU'LL NOTICE ALL YOUR EQUIPMENT HAS BEEN CUSTOM BUILT ACCORDING TO YOUR INDIVIDUAL "RAGTAG LEVELS" AND RATES OF MISFIT-ISM ∃NG-HEY∃. EACH ONE OF YOUR BASEBALL GLOVES COMES EQUIPPED WITH ITS OWN MINI-COMPUTER AND WIRELESS INTERNET CONNECTION.

UNAVOIDABLE, I'M AFRAID.

COACH, I'M ALREADY GETTING *SPAM!*

BEEP!

YOUR HELMETS WILL AUTOMATICALLY KEEP TRACK OF YOUR PERSONAL STATISTICS, AND THEY ARE EQUIPPED WITH CELLPHONES AND TEXT MESSAGING.

DORH⊖8AT

HEY!

JUST TESTING THE HELMET, LIS.

LOL :P

THE BASES HAVE BEEN FULLY *AUTOMATED* SO THEY CAN CLEAN THEMSELVES ∃GLAVIN!∃, AND I'VE DEVELOPED A SPECIAL *ENERGY DRINK* THAT WILL IMPROVE PERFORMANCE.

NYAH! IT'S LIKE MY HEART'S IN A BLENDER!

OH, DEAR. WELL, I KNEW THERE'D BE SOME TWEAKING.

LET'S *PLAY BASE!* ƎNG-HEY.ϟ

IT'S *BALL.*

BALL! PLAY *BALL!* OF COURSE.

THAT SATURDAY, THE LI'L TOPES FACE THE CAPITAL CITY CAR CRUSHERS...

GO BART'S TEAM! *WOO-HOO!*

HOMER, DID YOU HAVE TO BRING THE *ENTIRE* BUCKET O' SALSA?

SHERRI

YOU CAN'T HAVE BASEBALL WITHOUT SALSA, MARGE. IT'S AS *UN-AMERICAN* AS THE CUBANS WHO HAVE MASTERED THIS SPORT!

HEY, HOMER, A DAB OF THE SALSA WOULD REALLY MAKE OUR NACHOS SCRUM-DIDDLY-UMPTOUS!

GET SCRUM-DIDDLY-BENT, FLANDERS.

YOU BETCHA!

ALL RIGHT, KIDS, LET'S HAVE A GOOD CLEAN GAME FOR OL' UMPIRE GIL.

HEY, SPRINGFIELD WUSSY, SEE IF YOU CAN THROW ONE TO THE PLATE THIS TIME. A-HAW-HAW-HAW!

INITIATE TARGETING SEQUENCE.

INITIATED.

WHRRRRR!

WHRR!

BEEP!

TARGET LOCKED.

STRIKE!

WHAP!

OW! MY MASK! THEY MAKE YOU PAY FOR THESE.

WHIF!

THE 9TH INNING...

CR4CK!

ZOOM!
ZOOM!
ZOOM!
ZOOM!

| SPRINGFIELD LI'L TOPES | 18 |
| CAPITAL CITY CAR CRUSHERS | 0 |

NICE HIT, MILHOUSE! WE WON!

YEAH-YEAH-YEAH! W-WHERE'S MY ENERGY DRINK?

WHAT THE--?

TRIPLE PLAY, LOSER!

SMACK!

WELL DONE, MY EVIL MINIONS! WE NOW MOVE ON TO *THE CHAMPIONSHIP*! THERE, WE WILL CRUSH MY OLD NEMESIS, *PROFESSOR FRINK*, AND OUR EVIL WILL RULE THE LITTLE LEAGUE! *MWAH-HAHAHA!*

SINCE WE WON, CAN WE GET ICE CREAM?

YES! TO THE ICE CREAM PARLOR! *MWAH-HAHAHA!*

THE CHAMPIONSHIP GAME, TOP OF THE NINTH...

| WEST SPRINGFIELD ATOMIC BOMBS | 3 |
| SPRINGFIELD LI'L TOPES | 2 |

COME HERE, YOUNG BART, AND TRY THIS ON.

THIS AERODYNAMIC BASEBALL HELMET WILL HAVE YOU ROUNDING THIRD BEFORE THE FIRST BASEMAN CAN FINISH SCRATCHING HIMSELF. ‹NG-HEY›

BUT PROFESSOR, THIS IS AN UNTESTED PROTOTYPE. I COULD GET HURT.

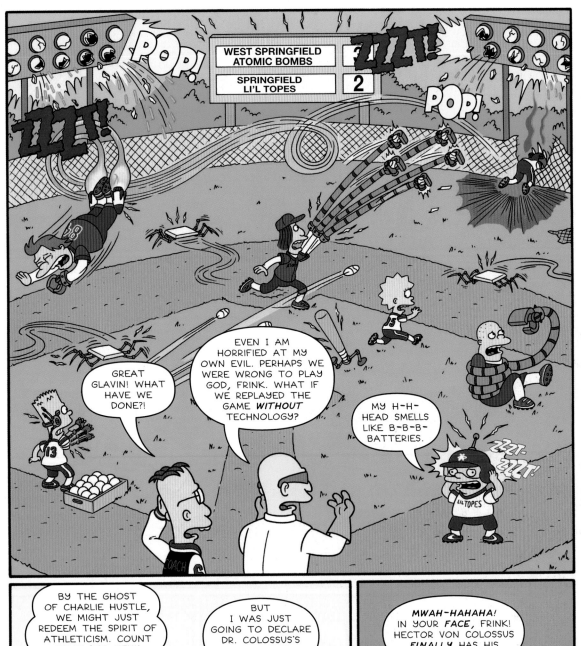

| WEST SPRINGFIELD ATOMIC BOMBS | ? |
| SPRINGFIELD LI'L TOPES | 2 |

POP!

ZZZT!

ZZZT!

POP!

GREAT GLAVIN! WHAT HAVE WE DONE?!

EVEN I AM HORRIFIED AT MY OWN EVIL. PERHAPS WE WERE WRONG TO PLAY GOD, FRINK. WHAT IF WE REPLAYED THE GAME *WITHOUT* TECHNOLOGY?

MY H-H-HEAD SMELLS LIKE B-B-B-BATTERIES.

ZZZT-ZZZT!

BY THE GHOST OF CHARLIE HUSTLE, WE MIGHT JUST REDEEM THE SPIRIT OF ATHLETICISM. COUNT ME IN ꓱNG-HEY!ꓱ

BUT I WAS JUST GOING TO DECLARE DR. COLOSSUS'S TEAM THE WINNER.

MWAH-HAHAHA! IN YOUR *FACE*, FRINK! HECTOR VON COLOSSUS *FINALLY* HAS HIS REVENGE!

ꓱSIGHꓱ ꓱNG-HEY!ꓱ

DON'T FEEL BAD PROFESSOR. YOU DID A GREAT JOB.

YEAH. BESIDES, I WON TEN BUCKS BETTING *AGAINST* OUR TEAM.

BART!

WELL, I DIDN'T THINK WE'D BEAT THE SPREAD.

YOU KIDS TAUGHT ME AN IMPORTANT LESSON TODAY. BASEBALL ISN'T ABOUT SPORTS-ENHANCING TECHNOLOGY. IT'S ABOUT *HEART* AND *GO-GETISM* AND SUCH!

IF I HADN'T LET MY MACHINES BLIND ME TO THAT, WE MIGHT HAVE WON TODAY. BUT NEVER AGAIN!

NOW LET'S ALL GET INTO THE TEAM FUSION-POWERED HOVER VAN AND HEAD BACK TO THE LAB FOR GENETICALLY MODIFIED MICROWAVED PEACH COBBLER AND VIRTUAL REALITY VIDEO GAMES! {WOO-HOY!}

WHAT ARE THEY CHEERING FOR? THEY LOST.

YOU THINK *FRINK'S TEAM* HAD TECHNOLOGY-- WAIT UNTIL WE PLAY THE *WORLD CHAMPIONSHIP* AGAINST THE *JAPANESE* TEAM NEXT WEEK!

YAY! YAY! YAY!

ONE WEEK LATER...

HOORAY!

HOME RUN!

CRACK!

JUST A MINUTE. THERE'S SOMETHING WRONG HERE--{GASP!} I *KNEW* IT!

TONY DIGEROLAMO
WRITER

JASON HO
PENCILS

MIKE ROTE
INKS

NATHAN HAMILL
COLORS

KAREN BATES
LETTERS

BILL MORRISON
EDITOR

21

LISA SIMPSON IN

THE THREE STAGES OF TEACHING

TOM PEYER WRITER **JOHN DELANEY** PENCILS **HOWARD SHUM** INKS **ART VILLANUEVA** COLORS **CHRIS UNGAR** LETTERS **BILL MORRISON** EDITOR

STAGE ONE: IDEALISM

FINE. IF *THAT'S* HOW SHE WANTS IT...

...LET'S DO SOME *REAL LEARNING!* WHO'S *WITH* ME?

ALL RIGHT. IT'S NOT *YOUR* FAULT IF NO ONE'S TRIED TO *INSPIRE* YOU!

TAKE TEN MINUTES AND WRITE A *POEM* ABOUT...LET'S SEE...

...YOUR *FAVORITE ANIMAL!*

OOH! *OOH!*

I LIKE MY LITTLE MUTT. HE'S GOT A FURRY BUTT!

HA HA HA HA HA

NO! A *REAL* POEM!

MISS *TEACHER?*

MY POEM'S *HURTING* MY EAR!

LET'S TRY AN *ART* PROJECT.

STAGE TWO: EXHAUSTION

23

A FEW MINUTES LATER...

NOW, CAREFULLY DIP YOUR PAPER INTO THE FLOUR PASTE...

HA!

FWAP!

HA HA HA HA HA HA

CLASS!

NO!

STOP!

¿GUH!?

STAGE THREE: SURRENDER

WELL, LISA? HOW'S YOUR LESSON PLAN COMING ALONG?

RAYMOND'S...WIFE... GETS...MAD...AT...HIS... MOTHER...WHEN...

MEH. TV GUIDE WILL DO.

STAGE THREE ALREADY?

THE END.

JAMES BATES
WRITER

LUIS ESCOBAR
PENCILS

PATRICK OWSLEY
INKS

NATHAN HAMILL
COLORS

KAREN BATES
LETTERS

BILL MORRISON
EDITOR

THE EXHIBITS HERE FEATURE *PRICELESS* ARTIFACTS.

I UNDER- STAND, SIR.

THERE'LL BE *ZERO TOLERANCE*. ONE OFFENSE AND YOU'RE SCHOOL IS ON *"THE LIST!"*

NO. NOT *"THE LIST!"*

SEE YA ON THAT LIST, SEYMOUR.

WELL, I KNOW WHEN I'M BEAT. I'LL JUST WAIT ON THE BUS.

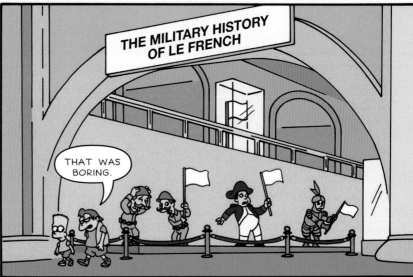

THE MILITARY HISTORY OF LE FRENCH

THAT WAS BORING.

RELICS OF THE OLD WEST

THIS IS FROM THE PONY EXPRESS. HMM, I WONDER HOW *MAD* THEY'D BE IF I SAT ON IT FOR JUST A SECOND?

OF THE VEST

FORGET *THAT!* YOU GOTTA SEE WHAT'S OVER *THERE*.

GAGH!:

THESE KIDS HAVE NO IDEA WHAT KIND OF BLACK MARK IT IS ON A *PRINCIPAL'S* PERMANENT RECORD TO GET ON "THE LIST."

THE COPS TOLD *ME* I'M ON A LIST.

THIS IS WORSE. WHEN WORD GETS OUT, SPRINGFIELD ELEMENTARY MIGHT BE BANNED FROM MUSEUMS *EVERYWHERE*.

I'M BETTER OFF WAITING FOR THE BAD NEWS HERE.

WHO KNOWS? MAYBE THE KIDS WILL SURPRISE YOU AND STAY OUT OF TROUBLE.

BACK WHERE THE ACTION IS...

MUST BE MY IMAGINATION PLAYING TRICKS ON ME.

¡GASP!¡

AH! MY LEG!

I *KNEW* IT! WHERE ARE YOU, YOU LITTLE HOODLUMS?

CLANG!

DO YOU WORK HERE?

HUH?

WE FOUND AN ANOMALY IN THE "HISTORY OF THE COMPUTER" EXHIBIT. YOUR PLAQUE SAYS THAT *COLOSSUS* WAS THE FIRST FULL-SIZED MACHINE WITH UTILIZABLE RAM.

BUT EVERYONE KNOWS IT WAS THE *MANCHESTER MARK I*.

WE BRING THIS TO YOUR ATTENTION BECAUSE WE ASSUME YOU ARE INTERESTED IN ARTI-*FACTS* NOT ARTI-*FICTIONS*.

WELL, OF COURSE, BUT...

ARTI-FICTIONS. ≀SNARK≀

KEEP MOVING OR WE'LL GET CAUGHT!

SLOW DOWN, MAN. MY LEG HURTS.

YOU'RE HOLDING ME BACK! LET'S GET THESE CUFFS OFF.

TARY HISTORY E FRENCH

THAT GUILLOTINE BLADE WILL CUT THE CHAINS. DO YOU THINK IT STILL WORKS?

THE HANDCUFFS DID.

ONE OF US HAS TO BE ON EITHER SIDE FOR THE BLADE TO CHOP THE CHAIN. GO AHEAD. CLIMB THROUGH.

NO WAY. *YOU* DO IT!

FINE, BUT IF I TRIP AND GET CUT IN HALF, I'M COMING BACK TO *HAUNT* YOU!

YOU WON'T TRIP.

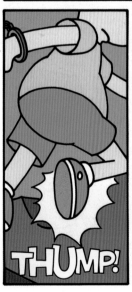

THUMP!

RATTLE!

I *KNEW* I'D TRIP!

HAW HAW!

IT'S MADE OUT OF *RUBBER!*

DUDE, I SO THOUGHT YOU WERE GONNA BE SLICED LIKE A PEPPERONI!

BOING!

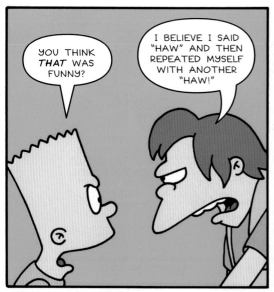

GRRR!

STOP IT, NELSON! THIS IS STUPID. WE SHOULD WORK *TOGETHER* BEFORE WE GET CAUGHT!

STOP RIGHT WHERE YOU ARE! YOU PUNKS ARE IN A LOT OF *TROUBLE!*

I THINK MY LEG IS BETTER. LET'S *RUN* FOR IT!

TOLD YOU!

UH-OH.

I THINK THAT'S SUPPOSED TO HAPPEN ANYWAY.

THAT CAKE IS MADE OF WAX, SON.

IT'S YUMMY. LIKE A CANDLE WITHOUT THE *BURNY PART.*

TWO DIPPY KIDS HANDCUFFED TOGETHER. I WON'T LET THEM *OUT-SMART* ME.

MAGIC: THEN AND NOW

LET'S HIDE IN HERE!

THIS STUFF RULES!

JUST MY LUCK. THERE'S FINALLY SOMETHING *COOL* ON A SCHOOL TRIP, AND I CAN'T EVEN *ENJOY* IT.

YOUR LUCK JUST GOT WORSE. THIS PLACE IS A *DEAD END,* AND THAT CURATOR DUDE IS PROBABLY ON HIS WAY.

I WISH THIS WAS THE *REAL* HARRY HOUDINI. HE COULD FIGURE A WAY OUT OF THIS.

WAIT! THAT'S ONE OF HOUDINI'S ACTUAL *TOOL KITS!*

SO?

HAVEN'T YOU EVER HEARD OF A *HOUDINI KEY*? THEY ARE LEGENDARY. A HOUDINI KEY CAN UNLOCK *ANY* LOCK.

HEY, WITH THAT WE COULD UNLOCK...OH, NOW I GET IT.

ALMOST THERE...A LITTLE HIGHER.

HURRY!

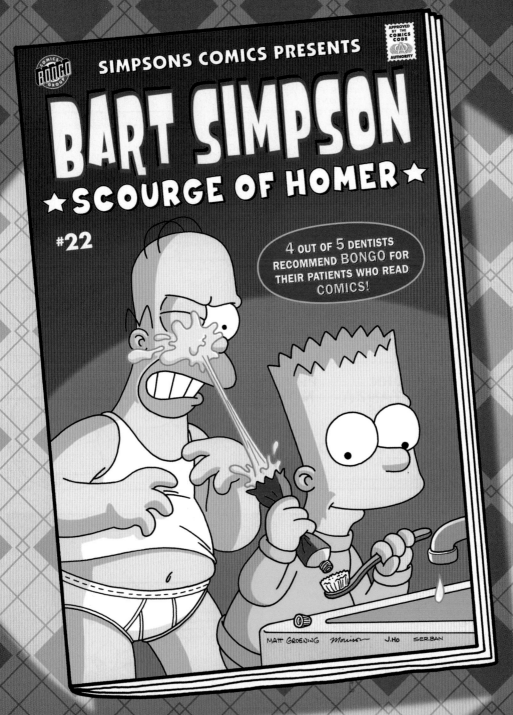

MATT GROENING presents BART SIMPSON IN

FINAL DETENTION

BART, IF MY CALCULATIONS ARE CORRECT, THE DETENTION I'M ABOUT TO WRITE FOR YOU WILL BE THE *ONE HUNDREDTH DETENTION* YOU'LL SERVE THIS SCHOOL YEAR!

YES!

WAIT, I MEAN *NO!*

ERIC **ROGERS** SCRIPT	JOHN **COSTANZA** PENCILS	PHYLLIS **NOVIN** INKS
NATHAN **HAMILL** COLORS	KAREN **BATES** LETTERS	BILL **MORRISON** EDITOR

AS PROUD AS I AM OF FINALLY BREAKING THE RECORD FOR *MOST DETENTIONS SERVED,* I CAN'T SERVE DETENTION TODAY!

I'LL MISS THE *TRY-OUTS* FOR THE SPRINGFIELD SKATEBOARD TEAM! THEY'RE GOING TO COMPETE AGAINST SHELBY-VILLE IN THE *X-TREME SPORT SHOWDOWN* IN THREE WEEKS!

PLEASE, PRINCIPAL SKINNER, I'LL DO **ANYTHING** IF YOU'D LET ME OFF THE HOOK FOR JUST TODAY!

BRRRING! BRRRING!

I'M SORRY, BUT YOUR NAME'S ALREADY ON THE SLIP. THERE'S **NOTHING** I CAN DO.

OH HELLO, MOTHER... WELL I'M IN THE MIDDLE OF **SCHOOL BUSINESS** HERE... NO, OF COURSE MY JOB ISN'T **MORE IMPORTANT** TO ME THAN YOUR **DENTURE PASTE**...

...WELL, HAVE YOU LOOKED IN THE **BUTTER DISH** IN THE REFRIGERATOR?

DETENTION

DELINQUENT: Bart Simpson

RIIIP!

MOTHER, JUST CALM DOWN. LET ME FINISH WHAT I'M DOING HERE AND I'LL CALL YOU RIGHT BACK...

ALL RIGHT, SIMPSON, NOW WHERE WERE WE-- **HEY!** WHERE DID HE GO?

WHOOOSH!

BRINGING DIRTY MAGAZINES TO SCHOOL, EH? LET'S SEE HOW *TRIBAL* YOU THINK DETENTION IS, MR. PRINCE!

GOODNESS NO, THIS IS AN *EDUCATIONAL* MAGAZINE! I READ IT FOR THE *ARTICLES*!

SELLING YOUR LUNCH IS AGAINST THE RULES, RALPH WIGGUM! YOU'RE GETTING *DETENTION*!

NELSON WAS GOING TO MAKE ME ALL HURTY IF I DIDN'T GIVE IT TO HIM!

LIKE I'D *EVER* DO THAT?

WE DIDN'T DITCH SCHOOL! WE CAUGHT AN INFECTIOUS FLU FROM A HUMMING-BIRD!

LIKELY STORY! I'M GOING TO *DOUBLE* MY PLEASURE BY GIVING YOU *BOTH* DETENTION!

SHERRI AND TERRI ARE IN TROUBLE, *TOO*? WHAT'S GOING ON AROUND HERE? ALL THE "GOOD" KIDS ARE GETTING DETENTION!

WHAT THE...?

EXIT

THAT DETENTION SLIP...

WHOOOSH!

DETENTION
DELINQUENT:
Bart Simpson

...LOOKS LIKE IT'S COMING RIGHT AT *ME*!

SWIIISH!

WHOA! THAT WAS *CLOSE*! WHO'S THIS DETENTION *FOR* ANYWAY?

BART?! THEN WHY IS IT COMING AFTER *ME*?

SHOO, DETENTION! GO AWAY! GO PICK ON SOMEBODY WHO *DESERVES* YOU!

SLAM!

WHEW! WHY WAS THAT DETENTION SLIP AFTER ME? I'VE NEVER HAD A DETENTION BEFORE, LET ALONE DONE ANYTHING TO *DESERVE* ONE...

WHICH IS *EXACTLY* WHY IT CHASED YOU!

HEAVYWEIGHT CHAMP *DREDERICK TATUM*?! WHAT ARE *YOU* DOING HERE?

I'M HERE TO EDUCATE YOU ON THE *COCOON OF PREPOSTEROUSNESS* THAT'S ABOUT TO ENGULF YOU AND THE *GOODY-TWO-SHOES CHILDREN* OF THIS SCHOOL!

LIBRARIAN

WHAT DO YOU MEAN?

THAT DETENTION SLIP WILL CONTINUE TO GET INNOCENT BOYS AND GIRLS IN TROUBLE UNTIL IT FINDS ITS *ORIGINAL INTENDED RECIPIENT!*

YOU MEAN IT'S LOOKING FOR *BART?!*

YES. THE SLIP WILL NEVER REST UNTIL BART SERVES THE DETENTION, MEANING NO ONE, NOT EVEN *YOU,* IS SAFE FROM ITS *FALSE IMPLICATIONS OF IMPROPRIETY!*

I HAVE TO FIND BART AND CONVINCE HIM TO SERVE THE DETENTION OR EVERYONE ELSE IS *DOOMED!*

GO THROUGH THE BACK DOOR TO GIVE THAT SLIP "THE SLIP"!

LIBRARIAN

ONE LAST QUESTION--WHAT EXACTLY ARE *YOU* DOING IN THE SCHOOL LIBRARY ANYWAY?

MUTTERMUTTER TITTER TITTER MUTTERMUTTER

AFTER CHEWING MY OPPONENT'S *EYE-BROWS* OFF IN MY LAST BOXING MATCH, I RE-EVALUATED MY CHOSEN PATH AND DECIDED TO CHANNEL MY *VIOLENT ENERGIES* INTO A MORE REWARDING CAREER AS A *SCHOOL LIBRARIAN.*

THERE WILL BE SILENCE IN THE LIBRARY! UNLESS, THAT IS, YOU'D LIKE TO MAKE THE ACQUAINTANCE OF *MR. DEWEY* AND *MR. DECIMAL!*

PSST! *BART!* IT'S *ME!* GET OVER HERE!

LISA! HOW'D YOU KNOW IT WAS ME?

WILD GUESS.

WHAT'S GOING ON? I CAN'T TALK TO YOU LONG. PRINCIPAL SKINNER'S LOOKING FOR ME.

IT WOULDN'T HAVE ANYTHING TO DO WITH THAT *DETENTION* HE GAVE YOU THIS MORNING, WOULD IT?

HOW DO *YOU* KNOW ABOUT THAT?

BART, THERE'S NO TIME OR REASONABLE WAY TO EXPLAIN THIS, BUT TRUST ME WHEN I TELL YOU *YOUR* DETENTION SLIP IS FLOATING AROUND THE SCHOOL GETTING INNOCENT KIDS IN TROUBLE!

PFFT, YEAH RIGHT! NEXT THING YOU'LL TELL ME IS DREDERICK TATUM IS THE SCHOOL LIBRARIAN!

BART, I'M *SERIOUS!* SEE FOR *YOUR-SELF!*

MILHOUSE, YOU KNOW THIS SCHOOL HAS A *STRICT POLICY* AGAINST YOUR UNDERPANTS SHOWING *ANYWHERE* OUTSIDE OF YOUR CLOTHES!

B-B-B-BUT I WAS JUST EATING MY LUNCH AND THEN NELSON CAME UP FROM BEHIND--!

SAVE IT FOR THE DETENTION HALL, BUSTER. NO ONE'S ABOVE THE *"BRITNEY ORDINANCE"*... ESPECIALLY *YOU!*

YOU'RE RIGHT, LISA! MILHOUSE IS IN TROUBLE BECAUSE SOMEONE ELSE GAVE HIM A WEDGIE! TALK ABOUT ADDING *INSULT TO INJURY!*

THE DETENTION SLIP'S COMING THIS WAY. YOU KNOW WHAT YOU HAVE TO DO, BART...

YEP! *RUN!*

NO, BART! YOU HAVE TO *TAKE THE DETENTION* OR NO ONE WILL BE SAFE FROM THE SLIP'S EVIL WAYS!

YOU *SEE?* IT'S TRYING TO GET ME IN TROUBLE AGAIN!

C'MON, LIS! WE'LL BE SAFE IN *HERE!*

THAT WAS *CLOSE!*

AYE! WHAT ARE YE DOIN' IN ME TOOL SHED? WILLIE'S GOT A HALF HOUR BEFORE TOILET POLISH DUTY AND ME "GUNS" NEED PUMPIN'!

WE'RE BEING ATTACKED BY A *SUPER-NATURAL* DETENTION SLIP THAT WON'T STOP UNTIL ITS THIRST FOR *AFTER-SCHOOL JUSTICE* IS QUENCHED!

ACH, WHY DIDN'T YOU SAY SO IN THE *FIRST PLACE?!* STAND ASIDE, WEE ONES!

THE END

45

BART SIMPSON in
BART BURGER

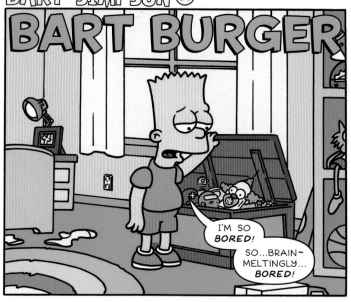

I'M SO *BORED!* SO...BRAIN-MELTINGLY... *BORED!*

≈HMMMPH≈ HAVEN'T USED THE OL' *KRUSTIE-TALKIE* IN A WHILE...

≈SKRIIK≈...AND A *KRUSTY-BACON SWIRLIE* WITH *BREADED BUTTER PATS...*

KLIK

BART, YOUR *WALKIE-TALKIE* IS PICKING UP THE *INTERCOM* AT THE *KRUSTYBURGER DRIVE-THRU!* ACCORDING TO *"BUSINESS WEEK FOR KIDS,"* KRUSTY WAS FORCED TO SELL ALL BUT ONE OF HIS *RADIO FREQUENCIES* BECAUSE--

HUH?

'NUFF SAID!

SLAAM!

...AND A *CLOWN-SIZE SHAKE* WITH A *CHEESE STRAW!*

YOU WANT *LARD* WITH THAT, *PORKY?*

SIR! NOT SINCE THE KLINGON *KORAX* SAID "THE ENTERPRISE SHOULD BE HAULED AWAY AS GARBAGE" HAVE I BEEN SO *INSULTED!*

WHA--?! I DIDN'T SAY ANYTHING!

BWA-HA-HA!

HA HA HA! I NEED TO GET *RINGSIDE* FOR *THIS!*

TOM PEYER SCRIPT   **JOHN COSTANZA** PENCILS   **HOWARD SHUM** INKS   **ART VILLANUEVA** COLORS   **KAREN BATES** LETTERS   **BILL MORRISON** EDITOR

THAT'LL BE ALL THE MONEY IN YOUR PANTS...

...AND YOUR PANTS!

WHA-?! THAT'S CRAZY!

...BUT I NEVER DISOBEYED A LOUDSPEAKER BEFORE, AND I SURE AIN'T GONNA START ON YOUR ACCOUNT, PIPSQUEAK!

EX-CU-USE ME?

TAKE!

AWWW, THIS IS TOO MUCH!

NOBODY SAID I'D HAVE TO HANDLE OLD PANTS!

I QUIT AGAIN!

...AND COME ON BACK FOR HAPPY HOUR! NICKEL BEERS FOR KIDS UNDER 12!

HEY! I SEE WHAT'S GOING ON!

YOU BETTER HAND THAT OVER, SIR!

EEE-YIKES!

MOMENTS LATER...

TRY OUR NEW FATTY MEAL, FOR PEOPLE ON THE GROW!

BWA-HA-HA!

STICK IT TO THE MAN, KID!

THE END

BART SIMPSON in
BAIT AND CACKLE

C'MON, BOY. I'M TAKING YOU ON A FATHER AND SON FISHING TRIP.

LIKE TO HELP YA OUT, HOMER. BUT I'M IN THE MIDDLE OF AN IMPORTANT... UH...BUSINESS MEETING.

GRAND THEFT KRUSTY

OH. I DIDN'T REALIZE YOU WERE IN THE MIDDLE OF--

--WAIT A MINUTE! YOU'RE ONLY TEN-YEARS-OLD! YOU DON'T HAVE BUSINESS MEETINGS!

SMACK!

I SAID, "GIMME THAT CAR!"

BART, GRAMPA NEVER TOOK ME ON FATHER AND SON TRIPS. AND WHEN I LOOK BACK AT ALL THE TIMES I'VE IGNORED YOU BECAUSE OF MY IMPORTANT BUSINESS MEETINGS AT MOE'S, I REALIZE THAT I'M BECOMING JUST LIKE--

SO YOU'RE JUST TAKING ME ON THIS FISHING TRIP OUT OF GUILT?

YEAH. NOW COME ON.

WHA--?!

OW! YOU RAN OVER MY CLOWN FEET!

CLICK!

TONY DIGEROLAMO
STORY

PHIL ORTIZ
PENCILS

PATRICK OWSLEY
INKS

NATHAN HAMILL
COLORS

KAREN BATES
LETTERS

BILL MORRISON
EDITOR

AW, MAN. I CAN'T BELIEVE I'M GOING TO BE STUCK OUT ON A LAME FISHING TRIP ALL DAY JUST BECAUSE HOMER WANTS TO BOND.

RENT-RENT-RENT YOUR BOAT
Boat Rental

ONE "FATHER AND SON SPECIAL," PLEASE.

THAT'LL BE THIRTY-NINE DOLLARS, SIR.

2 FOR 1 FATHER AND SON SPECIAL ONLY $39

HEY! YOU DIDN'T BRING ME OUT OF GUILT. YOU BROUGHT ME CAUSE IT'S CHEAP!

DON'T BE RIDICULOUS, BOY.

WITH TWO PEOPLE IN THE BOAT, WE'LL CATCH FOUR TIMES AS MANY FISH, RIGHT?

YAR. THAT BE TRUE.

PAY ATTENTION, BOY. LET ME SHOW YOU HOW TO BAIT A HOOK.

YEAH... HERE, KNOCK YOURSELF OUT.

BART! I'M TRYING TO TEACH YOU AN IMPORTANT LIFE SKILL. WHAT IF YOU GOT TRAPPED...UH...ON A RIVER OR A LAKE SOMEWHERE? HOW WOULD YOU SURVIVE?

I DON'T KNOW...

THE NEXT DAY...

HOMIE, WHAT'S THE MATTER?

I FAILED, MARGE. MY DAD NEVER SPENT ANY TIME WITH ME TO MAKE ME LIKE HIM, AND NOW BART IS GOING TO HATE ME FOR THE REST OF HIS LIFE. I'M A LOUSY FATHER.

REALLY? I JUST SAW BART, AND HE SEEMED PRETTY HAPPY ABOUT THE TRIP.

HERE HE COMES NOW. WHY DON'T YOU ASK HIM WHAT HE THOUGHT OF IT.

SON, DO YOU HATE ME FOR TAKING YOU ON THAT STUPID FISHING TRIP?

ARE YOU KIDDING? I HAD THE BEST TIME EVER!

HUH?

SURE, DAD! I JUST SIGNED US UP FOR THE TWO FOR ONE FATHER & SON SAFARI HUNT!

D'OH!

FATHER & SON

$39 SAFARI

THE END

BART SIMPSON (in) BIRTH OF A SALESMAN

BLECCH!

CLASS FUNDRAISER

IT'S THAT TIME OF YEAR AGAIN WHEN OUR CLASS RAISES MONEY FOR THE ANNUAL CLASS TRIP TO CAPITAL CITY.

AH, TIME FOR THE CLASS'S "SALESMAN OF THE YEAR" TO SHOW YOU ALL HOW IT'S DONE.

JAMES W. BATES
SCRIPT

JOHN DELANEY
PENCILS

PHYLLIS NOVIN
INKS

ART VILLANUEVA
COLORS

KAREN BATES
LETTERS

BILL MORRISON
EDITOR

HAH!

WHAT?

YOU ALWAYS HAVE YOUR DAD TAKE THE STUFF TO WORK AND TRICK HIS CO-WORKERS IN TO BUYING IT. THAT DOES NOT MAKE YOU A SALESMAN.

IF YOU DON'T HAVE YOUR DAD HELP YOU, I BET I CAN SELL MORE THAN YOU! THEN I'LL BE "SALESMAN OF THE YEAR!"

YOU'RE ON!

WAIT. IF THERE'S A BET, I'M IN, TOO.

OKAY, WHAT'S THE WAGER?

LOSERS HAVE TO DO THE WINNER'S HOMEWORK FOR A MONTH!

YOU GOT IT!

BUT MILHOUSE ALREADY DOES MY HOMEWORK.

ARE YOU IN SIMPSON, OR NOT?

OF COURSE I AM. I'M GOING TO HAWK THE HECK OUT OF WHATEVER WE SELL. BRING IT ON!

I HOPE IT'S CANDY.

WE CAN SELL CANDY IN OUR SLEEP.

DOESN'T MATTER WHAT IT IS. *I* CAN SELL *ANYTHING*.

HERE IT IS, CHILDREN. *THE LITTLE MISS BLUEBERRY COLLECTION!* WIND CHIMES, MINIATURE TEA SETS, AND THIMBLES... FEEL FREE TO COME UP AND SAMPLE THE MERCHANDISE!

THAT'S THE *LAMEST* THING EVER!

WHO'S IDEA WAS THIS?

I CAN'T SELL *THAT*.

UH, DUDES. WANNA CALL OFF THIS BET?

I'M WILLING TO IF BART IS...

THAT MIGHT BE FOR THE BEST.

I'M SURE GLAD YOU BOTH **CHICKENED** OUT OF THAT BET.

WHAT? ME, CHICKEN? NO WAY. LET'S **DOUBLE** THE BET!

LOSER DOES EVERYONE'S HOMEWORK FOR **TWO** MONTHS!

REMEMBER, YOU AGREED THAT HOMER CAN'T HELP YOU.

YEAH!

GIVE ME SOME CREDIT. A **MASTER SALESMAN** NEEDS NO HELP.

C'MON, HOMER! **PLEASE!** YOU **GOTTA** HELP ME?

BOY, I TOLD YOU, I'M NOT SELLING ANY FROUFY THINGS TO GUYS AT THE PLANT. THEY'D ALL LAUGH AT ME.

TELL YOU WHAT. WE'LL JUST **PAY YOUR WAY** FOR THE CLASS TRIP.

BART, DID YOU HEAR ME? I SAID I'D PAY. DID YOU MAKE SOME STUPID BET OR SOMETHING?

NO. I NEED TO **SELL** THIS STUFF.

UH...NO...I DIDN'T MAKE A BET! IT'S...PRIDE. I TAKE *PRIDE* IN DOING A GOOD JOB.

THAT'S IT. I'M GOING TO MOE'S. THE BOY IS TALKING *CRAZY*.

I THINK IT'S NICE THAT YOU WANT TO DO A *GOOD JOB*. BART, WITH THE RIGHT ATTITUDE, A PERSON COULD SELL ICE TO ESKIMOS.

THAT'D BE EASIER.

THE SELLING BEGINS...

PLEASE TAKE THAT AWAY! I DATED LITTLE MISS BLUEBERRY BEFORE THE WAR. THAT LITTLE MISS GOODY-GOODY BROKE MY HEART!

SPRINGFI
RETIREM
CASTL

YOU ARE CONFUSED, YOUNG NELSON MUNTZ. I SELL GOODS TO *YOU*. WHEN YOU ARE NOT STEALING THEM, THAT IS.

LITTLE MISS BLUEBERRY? WE WILL WORSHIP NO FALSE IDOLS HERE! GET THEE OUT OF MY CHURCH, SATAN!

WHAT KINDA JOKE YOU TRYIN' TO PULL? THIS SHOT GLASS HAS HOLES IN IT!

WORST SCHOOL FUNDRAISER EVER!

I'M SO EMBARRASSED.

WE COULDN'T *GIVE* THIS STUFF AWAY.

I HAVE TO GET A RABIES SHOT EVERY MORNING FOR THE NEXT NINE DAYS.

OH MY! I *LOVE* LITTLE MISS BLUEBERRY!

WIGSTOCK

GET WIGGY WITH IT!

HUH?

ALL THE LADIES ON MY BLOCK LOVE HER, TOO.

REALLY? WOULD YOU LIKE TO BUY SOME?

IT'S A SHAME YOU'RE NOT LITTLE GIRLS. I MEAN WHY WOULD *BOYS* BE SELLING WIND CHIMES AND THIMBLES? OOH, I'D BETTER CATCH MY BUS.

WIGSTOCK

I'M GONNA SELL ALL MY STUFF ON OLD LADY LANE!

NOT IF I GET THERE FIRST!

LADY! YOU FORGOT YOUR BAG!

GET WIGGY WITH IT!

SHE FORGOT HER WIG, HER PEARLS, HER LIPSTICK, A DRESS... HMM. WAIT A SECOND.

GET WIGGY WITH IT!

LATER, ON "OLD LADY LANE"...

PLEASE, MA'AM. BUY A WIND CHIME. PROCEEDS GO TO SICK KIDS.

NO. BUY FROM *ME*! PROCEEDS FROM MINE GO TO EVEN *SICKER* KIDS.

SORRY, BOYS. I ALREADY BOUGHT FROM THAT NICE, YOUNG LADY.

HUH.

WHO IS THAT?

IT'S *BART!*

UH-OH.

WHEN I CATCH YOU, I'M GONNA KICK YOUR LITTLE MISS *BUTT*-BERRY!

GIVE ME THAT WIG!

QUIT IT! LET ME GO!

WHAT ON EARTH?

I GOT THE LIPSTICK!

IN 'NAM I SAW A LOT OF DISTURBING THINGS, BUT THIS TAKES THE CAKE!

I DROP MOTHER OFF AT HER PINOCHLE GAME, AND I FIND...I FIND...**WHAT** HAVE I FOUND?

IT'S NOT OUR FAULT. IT'S LITTLE MISS BLUEBERRY'S!

THE NEXT DAY AT SCHOOL...

EVEN THOUGH SOME OF YOU DIDN'T SELL MORE THAN ONE OR TWO ITEMS, WE REACHED OUR GOAL AND MADE ENOUGH FOR OUR CLASS TRIP TO CAPITAL CITY!

WE DID IT!

AND IT'S ALL BECAUSE OF THE EFFORTS OF OUR **TOP SALESMAN**...**WENDELL!** HE SOLD MORE THAN EVERYONE ELSE **COMBINED!**

YAY!

GOOD JOB, WENDELL. HOW'D YOU DO IT?

MY DAD SOLD A BUNCH OF THAT JUNK AT WORK.

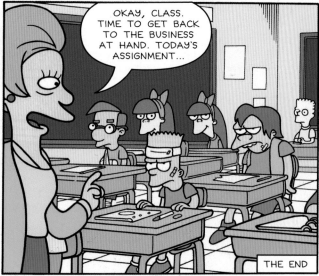

OKAY, CLASS. TIME TO GET BACK TO THE BUSINESS AT HAND. TODAY'S ASSIGNMENT...

THE END

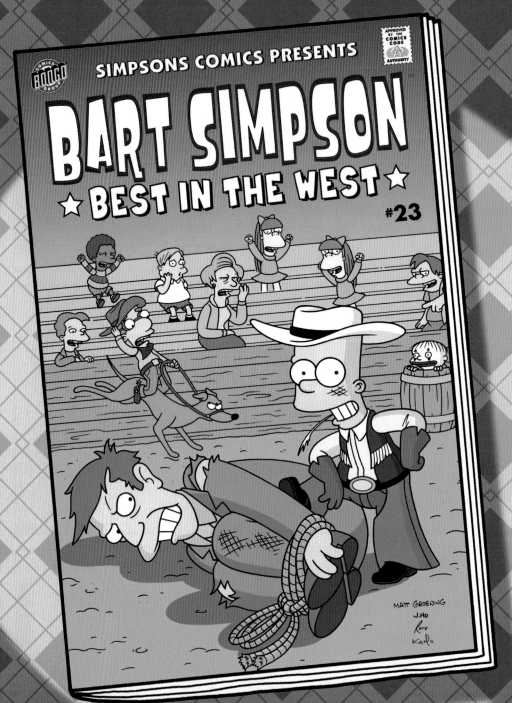

BART SIMPSON
in
BART vs. THE ONE-MAN SCHOOL

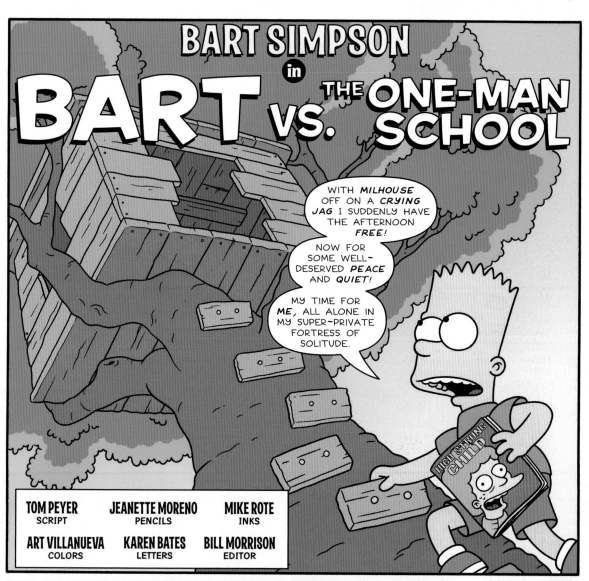

WITH *MILHOUSE* OFF ON A *CRYING JAG* I SUDDENLY HAVE THE AFTERNOON *FREE!*

NOW FOR SOME WELL-DESERVED *PEACE* AND *QUIET!*

MY TIME FOR *ME,* ALL ALONE IN MY SUPER-PRIVATE FORTRESS OF SOLITUDE.

HIGH-STRUNG CHILD

TOM PEYER
SCRIPT

JEANETTE MORENO
PENCILS

MIKE ROTE
INKS

ART VILLANUEVA
COLORS

KAREN BATES
LETTERS

BILL MORRISON
EDITOR

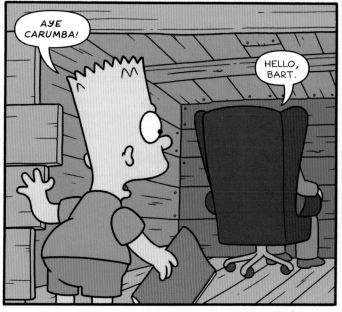

AYE CARUMBA!

HELLO, BART.

SKINNER?

FORGIVE ME MY *TRESPASS...*

...BUT MOTHER *INSISTED* YOU WOULDN'T WANT TO BE SEEN IN *PUBLIC* WITH YOUR *PRINCIPAL!*

SMART *LADY*.

HOW'D YOU GET THE *CHAIR* UP HERE?

NEVER *MIND* THAT. WE HAVE A *SITUATION*.

FRESH *INTELLIGENCE CHATTER* WARNS OF A SURPRISE FEDERAL *INSPECTION* OF *SPRINGFIELD ELEMENTARY!*

FEDS? OUCH!

YOU WOULDN'T WANT ANY KIDS MAKIN' YOU LOOK BAD IN FRONT OF *THEM*, SEYMOUR!

EXACTLY! BART, I'M NOT *PROUD* OF THE OFFER I'M ABOUT TO MAKE, BUT...

...I'M PREPARED TO MAKE *OBEDIENCE* WORTH YOUR WHILE, IF YOU KNOW WHAT I MEAN.

HUH?

I'LL *GREASE* YOUR *PALM!*

WHAT?

I'LL *PAY* YOU! *CASH!* JUST TO BE *GOOD* UNTIL AFTER THE *INSPECTION!*

HERE!

NOW!

GRAB IT! I WON'T TAKE ANY-THING LESS THAN *"YOINK"* FOR AN *ANSWER!*

FINE. YOINK. BUT HERE ARE MY *TERMS*, SEYMOUR...

I'LL KEEP BEHAVIN' ONLY AS LONG AS YOU KEEP PAYIN'.

SOON...

LET'S SEE...SIMPSON... SIMPSON...

NO, I DON'T SEE YOUR NAME ON THE LIST.

BART, CAN I *GO* YET? IT'S PAST MY BEDTIME!

I DECIDE THE BEDTIMES AROUND HERE.

WHY YOU--!

BART! WHERE'D *YOU* GET THE MONEY FOR ALL THIS JUNK?

UH-OH.

YOU WANT ME TO *HANDLE* HIM?

NOT *YET*, NELSON.

MILHOUSE, ⸨WHISPER⸩ ⸨WHISPER⸩ ⸨WHISPER⸩.

UHHH... *HERE*, MR. SIMPSON. THIS IS FROM *MR. SIMPSON*.

THE *OTHER* ONE.

WHAAAT?!

BART, I'M ONLY GOING TO SAY THIS ONCE.

CAN I BE IN *YOUR* POSSE? PLEASE?

I SWEAR I'LL BE LOYAL!

SEYMOUR! YOU'RE A DISGRACE!

WHAT IS IT *NOW*, MOTHER?

THREE DOLLARS?!?

WHEN DID RIFLING THROUGH YOUR POCKETS BECOME SUCH A PATHETIC WASTE OF TIME?

MOTHER, YOU HAVE NO *RIGHT*! I WAS *SAVING* THAT THREE DOLLARS FOR MY DATE WITH *EDNA*!

AHHH, LET THAT CHIPPIE FIND HER *OWN* FISH!

AND THEN SHE THREW MY *PANTS* IN MY FACE, TEMPORARILY *BLINDING* ME!

BUT WE MUSTN'T LET TALK OF *MOTHER* RUIN OUR DINNER, EDNA...

EDNA! WHAT DID I *SAY*? COME *BACK*! WE HAVEN'T EVEN HAD *APPETIZERS*!

ALL THE MORE FOR *YOU*--

BUMTOWN SOUP KITCHEN

--YOU CHEAPSKATE!

HEY, KEEP IT *MOVIN'*, DONALD TRUMP!

EGROOAAN

I *THOUGHT* I'D FIND YOU HERE, SEYMOUR.

OH. *HELLO*, BART.

CAN WE HURRY THIS UP? I LEFT MY *DAD* IN CHARGE OF THE *TREEHOUSE*.

RIGHT.

FORGIVE THE *ODOR*. MOTHER'S *GREED* REQUIRES ME TO FUNNEL ALL FUNDS TO MY *SHOE*.

IN FACT, TAKE THE *WHOLE DARN SHOE*. I JUST DON'T *CARE*.

YOU'RE A LITTLE *LIGHT* HERE, SEYMOUR! I'LL BE BACK *TOMORROW*!

HE'S BLEEDING ME *DRY!*

ASIDE FROM TEMPTING A CHILD INTO A LIFE OF *CORRUPTION*, WHAT DID I DO TO *DESERVE* THIS?

AND HOW DO I STEP *OFF* THIS MAD CAROUSEL?

WAIT A MINUTE!

PAYCHECKS! YES! TODAY IS THE SCHOOL'S *PAYDAY!*

THERE'S ENOUGH LOOT HERE TO BUY A *DOZEN* BART SIMPSONS!

I COULD NEVER *STEAL* IT, OF COURSE...

...BUT I COULD--*EARN* IT!

NYAAAHAHAHA!

SOON...

SKINNER! WHY'S ME PAY-CHECK GIRLIE-*PINK?*

THAT'S A DISMISSAL SLIP, *EX-*GROUNDSKEEPER WILLIE! WE'RE *LAYING* YOU *OFF!*

DON'T YOU DARE DO THIS, SKINNER, OR I'LL--

AIEEEE!

69

THAT'S *GROUNDS-KEEPER* SKINNER TO *YOU!*

NOW LEAVE THE PREMISES BEFORE I, ER, *DO* SOMETHING TO YOUR, UH, *GUTS!*

RUN, WILLIE! YA *FINALLY* MET YER *MATCH!*

HEH. THIS IS GOING NICELY *SO* FAR...

EDNA, CAN WE PATCH THINGS UP TONIGHT OVER *MARASCHINO LOBSTER* AT *THE GILDED TRUFFLE*?

REALLY? HOW CAN YOU *AFFORD* IT?

BY LAYING YOU OFF!

UHHDNUUH!

SLAAM!

LUNCHLADY DORIS, I DON'T QUITE KNOW HOW TO *SAY* THIS...

HIP-HIP HOORAY.

BART, LOOK! THERE'S THE *MAYOR'S LIMOUSINE!* AREN'T YA GONNA *WHIP* SOMETHIN' AT IT?

NAAAH, I *CAN'T.*

THIS *SMELLS!* SKINNER'S *ALWAYS* WATCHING ME NOW! IN CLASS, ON THE GROUNDS, IN THE LUNCHROOM, ON THE BU--

I SAID NO TALKING!

REMEMBER, BART! BE GOOD!

WHAT I DO ON *MY* TIME IS *MY* BUSINESS, SEYMOUR.

BART, FOR THE LAST TIME, TELL ME WHERE ALL THAT *MONEY'S* COMING FROM. YOU'RE NOT SELLING *GRIT,* ARE YOU?

IT'S NOTHING *LIKE* THAT, MOM! I *PROMISE!*

THEN *WHAT?* PLEASE! I *HAVE* TO KNOW! I'M YOUR *MOTHER!*

DON'T SNITCH ON THE POSSE, BOY!

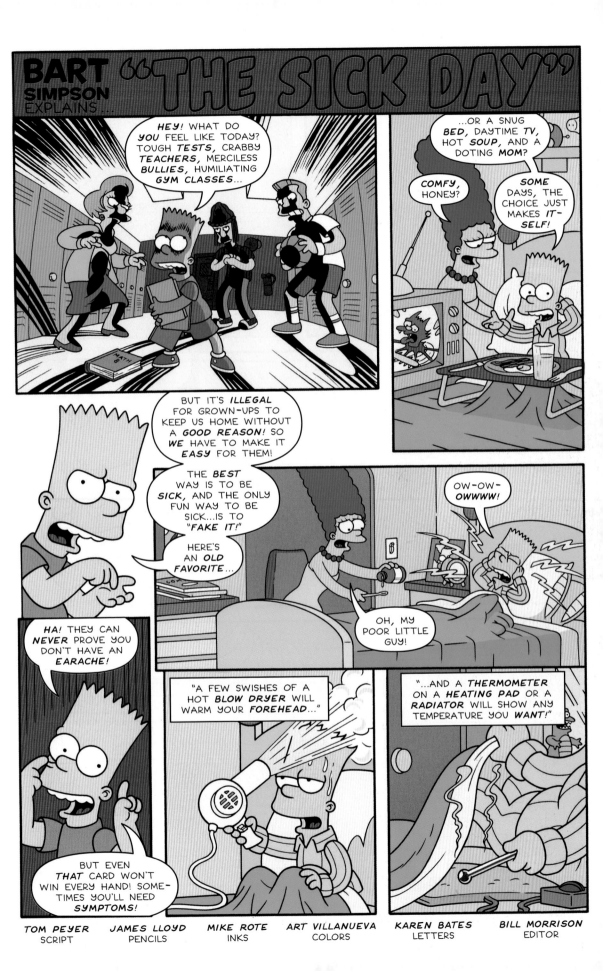

BART SIMPSON EXPLAINS... "THE SICK DAY"

HEY! WHAT DO YOU FEEL LIKE TODAY? TOUGH TESTS, CRABBY TEACHERS, MERCILESS BULLIES, HUMILIATING GYM CLASSES...

MATH

...OR A SNUG BED, DAYTIME TV, HOT SOUP, AND A DOTING MOM?

COMFY, HONEY?

SOME DAYS, THE CHOICE JUST MAKES IT-SELF!

BUT IT'S ILLEGAL FOR GROWN-UPS TO KEEP US HOME WITHOUT A GOOD REASON! SO WE HAVE TO MAKE IT EASY FOR THEM!

THE BEST WAY IS TO BE SICK, AND THE ONLY FUN WAY TO BE SICK...IS TO "FAKE IT!"

HERE'S AN OLD FAVORITE...

OW-OW-OWWWW!

OH, MY POOR LITTLE GUY!

HA! THEY CAN NEVER PROVE YOU DON'T HAVE AN EARACHE!

"A FEW SWISHES OF A HOT BLOW DRYER WILL WARM YOUR FOREHEAD..."

"...AND A THERMOMETER ON A HEATING PAD OR A RADIATOR WILL SHOW ANY TEMPERATURE YOU WANT!"

BUT EVEN THAT CARD WON'T WIN EVERY HAND! SOME-TIMES YOU'LL NEED SYMPTOMS!

TOM PEYER
SCRIPT

JAMES LLOYD
PENCILS

MIKE ROTE
INKS

ART VILLANUEVA
COLORS

KAREN BATES
LETTERS

BILL MORRISON
EDITOR

The SIMPSONS in SPECIAL DELIVERY

I WONDER WHAT IT IS?

IT'S BIG. IT COULD BE ANYTHING. C'MON, LET'S GET IT OPEN.

TO: THE SIMPSONS c/o HOMER SIMPSON

THIS PACKING TAPE IS TOUGH TO RIP.

DON'T WORRY, I KNOW WHERE HOMER HIDES THE BLOW TORCH.

WAIT! THE LABEL SAYS IT'S FOR YOUR FATHER.

CARE OF HOMER SIMPSON? OH!

HUH?

TO: THE SIMPSONS c/o HOMER SIMPSON

BUT IT COULD BE...

...SOMETHING WONDERFUL.

TO: THE SIMPSONS c/o HOMER SIMPSON

JAMES BATES SCRIPT   **JOHN DELANEY** PENCILS   **HOWARD SHUM** INKS   **ART VILLANUEVA** COLORS   **KAREN BATES** LETTERS   **BILL MORRISON** EDITOR

WHILE MOM IS OUTSIDE, WE COULD OPEN THE BOX AND THEN SEAL IT BACK UP BEFORE SHE NOTICES.

I'MBA WAYBA AHEABA YOUBA.

GOBB IT!

UH-OH! WE'RE SNAGGED!

ALL THAT TROUBLE...AND FOR *THIS*?

WHAT A GYP!

YOU OPENED IT!

YEAH, AND, BOY, ARE WE SORRY.

...EATEN ANY OF MY... *DIAPERS*?

IT SAYS HERE YOU ENTERED A "FAMILY SWEEP-STAKES" AND ARE THE WINNER OF A YEAR'S SUPPLY OF WUVS.

I REMEMBER THAT. I WAS TRYING TO WIN A SANDWICH.

GOOD ONE, HOMER. YOU FINALLY WIN SOME-THING, AND IT'S POOPY-PANTS!

WELL, I KNOW SOMEONE WHO'S HAPPY.

D'OH!

COO-COO!

THE END

BART SIMPSON IN KWIK-E-BART

HEY, APU! *HOT* ENOUGH FOR YA?

DING LING

HOW 'BOUT THOSE *SPRINGFIELD ISOTOPES?*

I SEE THE JERKS IN *CONGRESS* ARE UP TO THEIR OLD TRICKS--

--APU? WHERE *ARE* YOU?

BART SIMPSON, OPEN UP THE *DOOR,* PLEASE! THANK YOU VERY *MUCH!*

BAM! BAM! BAM!

OHHH, WHY DID I *EVER* INSTALL THE *SOUNDPROOFING* AND THE *UNBREAKABLE TRIPLE TIME-LOCK?*

TOM PEYER SCRIPT · **JAMES LLOYD** PENCILS · **MIKE ROTE** INKS · **NATHAN HAMILL** COLORS · **KAREN BATES** LETTERS · **BILL MORRISON** EDITOR

YOUNG MAN! THIS CAVIAR YOU SOLD ME IS WELL PAST ITS *FRESHNESS* DATE

HEY, *I* DON'T WORK HERE!

WELL, OF *COURSE* YOU DO! I DON'T SEE ANYONE *ELSE*!

·Checks
·Credit Cards
·Food Stamps

HMMM...

IF *I* WERE YOU, LADY, I WOULDN'T TALK ABOUT *FRESHNESS* DATES!

NOW *BEAT* IT BEFORE I CALL THE *LAW*!

WELL, I *NEVER*!

KWIK-E-MART

GIV

ecks

HEH! *THIS* COULD BE FUN.

I'LL NEED TO SEE SOME *PROOF OF AGE* FOR THAT *BEER*.

AWWW, BART--!

IT'S THE *LAW*, DAD!

CRATE -O- Duff

KWIK -E-

LOOKS *FAKE* TO *ME*!

DON'T COME BACK 'TIL YOU'RE 21!

YESSIR.

RIP!

CRATE -O- Duff

CRATE -O- Duff BEER

THE END

BART! DIDN'T YOU GET *ANY* SLEEP? WHAT WERE YOU *DOING* ALL NIGHT?

ZZZZ

SNUCK DOWNSTAIRS... SAW HOMER ASLEEP WITH TV ON... WATCHED 'TIL DAWN.

CARSON DALY... *REALLY* LETTING SELF GO...

BART, *WAIT!*

THAT'S NOT OUR BUS!

BART SIMPSON in GRAMPA BART

LOOK WHO'S SPENDIN' THE *DAY* WITH US! IT'S MY *GRANDSON!*

RIGHT *HERE,* BART!

WHA--?

AAAIIEEE!

TOM PEYER SCRIPT   JOHN COSTANZA PENCILS   HOWARD SHUM INKS   ART VILLANUEVA COLORS   KAREN BATES LETTERS   BILL MORRISON EDITOR

SEVEN HOURS LATER...

BART!

OH, WHERE HAVE YOU *BEEN?* WE WERE WORRIED *SICK!*

YOU *SHOULDA* BEEN! THAT BINGO HALL WAS AN *ICEBOX!* SOMEBODY'LL CATCH THEIR *DEATH!*

BINGO HALL?

AND THE *SNACK BAR!* CAN YOU BELIEVE THEY ACTUALLY *SELL* BOTTLES OF *WATER?*

AND PEOPLE *BUY* THEM?

BART! GET WITH THE TIMES!

YOUR FATHER'S *RIGHT,* DEAR! YOU *DO* SEEM KIND OF...*OLD!* DO YOU *FEEL* OK?

≥GROAAAN≤ DON'T GET ME *STARTED!* MY RIGHT HIP'S *KILLING* ME...

...AND I'D GIVE MY *XBOX* TO BE ABLE TO SLEEP 'TIL *SUN-UP!*

I'M CALLING DR. HIBBERT! YOU GET STRAIGHT UP TO BED!

AWWW! CAN'T I STAY UP AND WATCH "*JAG*"?

?

THE END

BART SIMPSON in FLU SHOT

WE'RE ALMOST THERE.

"FREE CANDY DAY!" IT SOUNDS TOO GOOD TO BE TRUE, MOM!

WAIT A MINUTE. THIS ISN'T THE WAY TO CANDYOPOLIS! *THIS* IS THE WAY TO... *DR. HIBBERT'S OFFICE!*

IT'S TIME TO GET YOUR *FLU SHOTS!*

FLU VACCINATION DAY!

OH NO!

NEEDLES?! BUT YOU SAID IT WAS "FREE CANDY DAY!"

YOU SOLD US OUT, MOM! IF WE CAN'T TRUST YOU, WHO *CAN* WE TRUST?

I'M SORRY, BUT IT'S FOR YOUR OWN GOOD.

JAMES BATES SCRIPT **JASON HO** PENCILS **MIKE ROTE** INKS **NATHAN HAMILL** COLORS **KAREN BATES** LETTERS **BILL MORRISON** EDITOR

SUCKER! THE PATENTED *SPIN-O-RAMA!*

HUH? WHAT ARE YOU--?!

AH, IT LOOKS LIKE YOU'RE NEXT IN LINE, LISA.

I FEEL BAD FOR YOU. *I REALLY, REALLY DO.*

YOU TRICKED ME!

A FEW MOMENTS LATER...

AH HEE HEE HEE. BAD NEWS, BART. WE JUST USED UP THE LAST OF THE VACCINE. YOUR SISTER GOT THE LAST SHOT.

WE'LL HAVE TO RESCHEDULE YOURS ON ANOTHER DAY.

FLU VACCINE DAY

WOO-HOO!

A FEW DAYS LATER...

:GROAN: I FEEL *AWFUL.* :COUGH: :HACK!: I WISH I HAD GOTTEN THAT FLU SHOT.

WHERE IS EVERYONE GOING?

TODAY REALLY *IS* "FREE CANDY DAY" AT CANDYOPOLIS, BUT NOW THAT YOU HAVE THE FLU, YOU HAVE TO STAY HOME IN BED. SORRY.

I FEEL BAD FOR YOU, BART. *I REALLY, REALLY DO!*

THE END

MATT GROENING presents **BART SIMPSON** in **BART'S GOT SPIRIT!**

JAMES BATES	JOHN DELANEY	HOWARD SHUM	ART VILLANUEVA	KAREN BATES	BILL MORRISON
SCRIPT	PENCILS	INKS	COLORS	LETTERS	EDITOR

SUPERINTENDENT CHALMERS, I STILL THINK THIS IS A *BAD IDEA*.

STOP THINKING, SKINNER.

THE STATE HAS MANDATED THAT ALL ELEMENTARY SCHOOLS MUST ORGANIZE AN ATHLETICS SQUAD. THIS SCHOOL IS ORDERED TO INSTITUTE AN *AFTERSCHOOL FOOT-BALL PROGRAM.*

I UNDERSTAND THAT, BUT I'M NOT SURE WE HAVE THE *RAW TALENT* TO MAKE A COMPETITIVE TEAM.

OOOH! MY SPLEEN!

THE STATE BOARD OF EDUCATION SAYS YOU *NEED* A TEAM, AND THEY'RE COMING HERE IN TWO WEEKS TO WATCH YOU SCRIMMAGE WITH SHELBYVILLE ELEMENTARY.

BUT...

JUST DON'T *EMBARRASS* ME ...*COACH!*

PTWEET!

DON'T WORRY, *COACH*. HOW COULD ANY TEAM WITH *ME* ON IT EMBARRASS *YOU*?

YOU'RE NOT EVEN GOING TO GET THE CHANCE TO TRY, BART.

YOU WON'T EMBARRASS ME OR THIS TEAM BECAUSE YOU WON'T BE ON IT. *YOU'RE CUT!*

LATER THAT NIGHT...

CUT FROM AN ELEMENTARY SCHOOL TEAM? JUST WHEN I THOUGHT MY LOWERED EXPECTATIONS COULDN'T GET ANY LOWER.

I DIDN'T EVEN TRY OUT. SKINNER WOULDN'T LET ME!

HRMMM...THIS JUST DOESN'T SEEM RIGHT.

AS MUCH AS BART PROBABLY DESERVES HIS COMEUPPANCE, THE STATE'S MANDATE SAYS THAT EVERY CHILD WHO *WANTS* TO BE A PART OF THE PROGRAM *MUST* BE A PART OF IT.

YOU MEAN, EVEN IF HE STINKS, BART CAN'T BE CUT? WOO-HOO!

HEH-HEH, SKINNER IS GONNA BE SO MAD.

AT THE NEXT PRACTICE...

I HAVE IT ON GOOD AUTHORITY THAT YOU CAN'T CUT MY SON! HE SAYS HE WANTS TO BE PART OF THIS PROGRAM AND SO YOU HAVE TO LET HIM.

LOOKS LIKE I MADE THE TEAM.

BART, TAKE IT FROM ME, YOU SHOULDN'T HAVE YOUR MOTHER FIGHT YOUR BATTLES FOR YOU.

HOWEVER, SHE'S RIGHT. I HAVE TO KEEP YOU IN THE **PROGRAM**, SO WELCOME TO...

...THE CHEERLEADING SQUAD!

YOU'RE WELCOME TO BE IN THE PROGRAM AS LONG AS YOU LIKE. JUST PUT DOWN THOSE BALLS AND SCURRY OVER AND JOIN THE PUMETTES.

HUH?!

HAW HAW!

THIS WON'T STOP ME. DO YOU THINK I CAN'T CAUSE TROUBLE AS A CHEERLEADER?

I KNOW YOU CAN, BUT I'LL JUST LET THE CHEERLEADING COACH DEAL WITH YOUR TOMFOOLERY.

AH...THERE'S THE COACH NOW. WHY, IT'S **ASSISTANT SUPERINTENDENT LEOPOLD**.

I WANT TO SEE SPIRIT, AND I MEAN S-P-I-R-I-T, OUT OF YOU MAGGOTS.

YOU THINK YOU'RE MAN ENOUGH TO BE A PUMETTE, SIMPSON?

I GUESS SO. I'LL TRY.

THERE IS NO "TRY," THERE IS ONLY "CHEER." NOW GO PUT ON THIS UNIFORM.

93

MINUTES LATER...

SIMPSON, YOU LOOK...

...SO...

...COOL!

NOW THAT WE'VE GOT A STUD ON THE SQUAD, WE CAN BUILD A PYRAMID!

WOULDN'T THAT BE A "CHEER"-AMID?

OH, BART. YOU'RE SO FUNNY.

MY SISTER THINKS YOU'RE CUTE, BUT I DON'T. I THINK YOU'RE *DREAMY*.

SKINNER REALLY GOT YOU THIS TIME.

I DON'T THINK SO. CHEERLEADING HAS ITS PERKS.

SIMPSON! THIS IS NOT TALK TIME, IT'S CHEER TIME. GET OVER THERE!

YES, SIR!

PERKS?

CHINS UP! SUCK IN THOSE GUTS. I'VE NEVER SEEN A SORRIER GROUP OF RECRUITS IN MY LIFE!

WAIT...I'M SORRY. I MAY LOOK AND SOUND TOUGH ON THE OUTSIDE, BUT I'M REALLY JUST A BIG CHEERLEADER AT HEART.

YOU'RE GOING TO BE THE *BEST DARNED PEP SQUAD* THIS SCHOOL HAS EVER SEEN! C'MON, IT'S TIME TO SHOW ME WHAT YOU'VE GOT!

LATER AT HOME...

I'M HAVING SECOND THOUGHTS ABOUT FORCING PRINCIPAL SKINNER TO PUT YOU ON THE TEAM. IT LOOKS LIKE FOOTBALL IS TOO ROUGH FOR YOU.

NONSENSE. PLAYING FOOTBALL WILL MAKE A MAN OUT OF HIM. A LITTLE INTENTIONAL ROUGHING IS GOOD FOR A BOY!

BART, ARE YOU GOING TO TELL THEM OR SHOULD I?

I'M NOT ON THE TEAM.

I NEED A BEER.

IF YOU'RE NOT ON THE TEAM, WHERE DID YOU GET SO BEATEN UP?

AT PRACTICE.

WHAT KIND OF PRACTICE?

CHEERLEADER PRACTICE. I'M A PUMETTE.

MARGE... TAKING LIFE SAVINGS...GOING TO MOE'S...MUST... FORGET... SHAME.

NEVER MIND YOUR FATHER, I THINK CHEER-LEADING IS WORTH A FEW BRUISES IF IT MAKES YOU HAPPY.

IT DOESN'T MATTER. I'M QUITTING TOMORROW.

THE NEXT DAY...

I FIGURED I SHOULD RETURN THIS.

I DIDN'T ASK YOU TO QUIT.

BUT I STINK!

SURE YOU DO! BUT YOU STINK WITH *SPIRIT!*

YOU REALLY WANT ME TO STAY?

C'MON, GIRLS. TELL HIM! *WHO'S OUR FAVORITE PUMETTE*?

B-A-R-T! BART-BART-BART!!!

GAME DAY!

HOMER, TAKE THAT OFF.

WE'RE HERE TO SUPPORT BART. HE TOLD ME HE'S VERY EXCITED ABOUT THE PUMETTE *HALF TIME EXTRAVAGANZA*, AND I'M PROUD OF HIM.

I'M JUST DOING WHAT DETROIT LION FANS HAVE BEEN DOING FOR YEARS.

GO PUMAS

SUPERINTENDENT CHALMERS, IT'S TIME TO EVALUATE YOUR ATHLETICS PROGRAM. LET'S BEGIN.

THE GAME

WHIFF!

YAAAH!

:GULP!:

THE PUPPY IS HURT!

SHELBYVIL 40

SPRINGFIE 0

I CAN'T TAKE ANYMORE. LET'S JUST STOP THIS FIASCO, AND CALL IT A DAY.

YOU CAN'T STOP IT YET. YOU HAVEN'T SEEN OUR HALF TIME SHOW.

I'M SORRY, YOUNG MAN. NOBODY WANTS TO SEE ANY HALF TIME SHOW.

THAT'S NOT TRUE. THESE KIDS WORKED HARD. I WANT TO SEE IT, AND SO SHOULD YOU!

HE'S RIGHT. IT'S PART OF THE PROGRAM. WE MAY AS WELL WATCH IT...

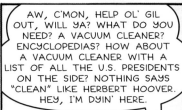

TONY DIGEROLAMO — SCRIPT   JASON HO — PENCILS   PHYLLIS NOVIN — INKS   ART VILLANUEVA — COLORS   KAREN BATES — LETTERS   BILL MORRISON — EDITOR

I FIND YOUR LACK OF APPRECIATION FOR "THE AVENGERS" CONTINUITY APPALLING IN THE EXTREME. CLEARLY, TODAY'S EDUCATIONAL SYSTEM IS ABOUT AS EFFECTIVE AS BEN AFFLECK'S ONE-DIMENSIONAL PORTRAYAL OF *DAREDEVIL*.

NOW GET OUT OF MY STORE BEFORE YOU DOWNGRADE THAT COPY OF "GREEN LANTERN VS. DICK CHENEY" FROM NEAR MINT TO FINE CONDITION WITH YOUR SWEATY FINGERPRINTS.

Type:	Comic Book Nerd
Latin Name:	Sequentialartum Connoisseurius Sarcasticus
Habitat:	Comic book stores, comic book conventions, Krusty Burger

I'M NOT YOUR MOMMY, AND I DON'T KNOW THE ANSWERS TO THE QUIZ. I ONLY KNOW THAT YOURS ARE WRONG. I DON'T KNOW WHY YOUR GRADES ARE SLIPPING. NOW LET'S JUST RUN OUT THE CLOCK AND STARE INTO SPACE FOR THE LAST TWENTY MINUTES OF THE SCHOOL DAY.

Type:	Teacher Dingus
Latin Name:	Eyerollum Fedupicus
Habitat:	Classrooms, faculty lounges, therapist couch

NEVER BREAK THE LAW, KID, OR YOU'LL REGRET IT. THE LAW IS ALL ABOUT PERSONAL RESPONSIBILITY. HEY, YOU SEE MY GUN ANYWHERE? I THOUGHT I LEFT IT HERE. OH WELL, IT'LL TURN UP.

Type:	Police Dork
Latin Name:	Lazias Protectorum Corruptus
Habitat:	Donut Shops, police stations, on his butt

WHEN I WAS A LITTLE DUDE, I NEVER STUDIED AND LOOK WHERE I AM! I CAN EAT WHATEVER I WANT! (WHEN I HAVE THE MONEY.) AND I CAN TRAVEL ALL OVER THE WORLD! (IF I HAD ANY MONEY.) I COULD'VE DONE ANYTHING WITH MY LIFE, IF...

...UH... WHAT WERE WE TALKIN' 'BOUT AGAIN?

Type:	Bus Schmoe
Latin Name:	Vehicularum Operatus Cannabis
Habitat:	Beanbag chairs, dumpsters, his parents' basement

WHY ARE YOU SQUANDERING ALL YOUR TIME WITH PLAY AND HAPPINESS? THAT WON'T GET YOU ANY RICHER! IF YOU DON'T START PINCHING EVERY PENNY NOW, YOU'LL NEVER AFFORD A CAVERNOUS, EMPTY MANSION TO RATTLE AROUND IN DURING YOUR FINAL DAYS!

Type:	Millionaire Doofus
Latin Name:	Greedae Consumicus
Habitat:	Country clubs, manor houses, mausoleums that resemble manor houses

SO ALONE... SO VERY ALONE.

Type:	Ding-dong Divorcée
Latin Name:	Spinsterus Oldmaidicus
Habitat:	Singles bars, internet dating chat rooms, one bedroom apartments

IT IS ONLY THROUGH THE STUDY OF NERDS BOTH PAST AND PRESENT THAT WE CAN TRULY UNDERSTAND AND BULLY THEM. I'M NELSON MUNTZ. GOOD NIGHT.

NOW, WHERE WAS I? OH YEAH...GIVE ME YOUR LUNCH MONEY OR I'LL INTRODUCE YOU TO MR. KNUCKLES! HAW HAW!

THE END

SHERRI & TERRI in THE KISS OF BLECCH!

TONY DIGEROLAMO SCRIPT **JASON HO** PENCILS **MIKE ROTE** INKS **ART VILLANUEVA** COLORS **KAREN BATES** LETTERS **BILL MORRISON** EDITOR

"LITTLE DID I KNOW, THOSE TWO CACKLING HENS, SHERRI AND TERRI, WERE PLAYING *SPIN THE BOTTLE* RIGHT BEHIND ME!"

YOU'RE IT, BART SIMPSON!

NYAAAAH!

AND WE'RE GOING TO KISS YOU!

NO WAY, MAN! YOU'LL NEVER GET YOUR COOTIE-FILLED LIPS ON ME!

YES WE WILL!

SO YOU GOTTA HIDE ME IN YOUR LOCKER! I'LL DO ANYTHING! I'LL EVEN GIVE YOU BACK THE STUFF I STOLE THAT YOU DON'T KNOW ABOUT!

SORRY, BART, IF THE BOTTLE POINTED TO YOU, THEY HAVE TO KISS YOU. IT'S *THE LAW*. BESIDES, IT'S TIME FOR MY TWO O'CLOCK BULLYING.

RIGHT ON TIME.

I PRIDE MYSELF ON PUNCTUALITY.

I GOTTA FIND A PLACE!

WELL, ANGEL, NOW THAT HOMER TOOK THE REST OF THE FAMILY TO MOUNT SPLASHMORE AND ASKED ME TO BABYSIT, WHAT DO YOU WANT TO DO TODAY? ANYTHIN' YOU WANT! THE SKY AND, UH, $17 IS THE LIMIT!

GA-GA-GOO! HEE-HEE!

BABY BRAND OATMEAL

NOW 38% FEWER RAT DROPPINGS!

:SNIFF-SNIFF!: WHEW! YOU SMELL THAT? THAT'S SOME INTERESTIN' STINK THERE THAT PROBABLY SHOULDN'T COME FROM NO BABY.

SUCK!

SUCK!

OH, I GET IT. YEAH, HOMER'S GOTTA LOT OF WEIRD AROMAS SURROUNDIN' HIM.

I THOUGHT I RECOGNIZED THAT SMELL FROM THE BAR.

SUCK! SUCK!

NORMALLY, THE CIGARETTE SMELL, Y'KNOW, SORTA DROWNS IT OUT AND ALL.

C'MON, ANGEL. HERE COMES SONNY TO THE TOLLBOOTH. HEY, C'MON, YOU NORMALLY LOVE THIS CRAP. WHY AIN'TCHA EATIN' IT?

OH, I SEE, YOU WANTED A LITTLE SUGAR THERE ON YOUR OATMEAL. HOMER MUST'VE TOOK THE SUGAR BAG WITH 'EM TO EAT ON THE LOG FLUME. THAT'S ALWAYS BEEN HIS DREAM. OR AT LEAST, AFTER A FEW BEERS, THAT'S WHAT HE *SAYS*. C'MON, WE'LL GO BORROW A CUP OF SUGAR.

SUGAR

AS MR. RITZFIELD'S ATTORNEY, I'D LIKE TO THANK YOU ALL FOR COMING TO THE READING OF THE WILL. OL' GIL IS HOPING FOR SOMETHING TOO. HEH-HEH. I'LL TAKE ANYTHING, EVEN THE FOOD LEFT IN THE FRIDGE! C'MON, THE WOLVES ARE AT OL' GIL'S DOOR!

KNOCK! KNOCK! KNOCK!

EXCUSE ME, SIR. THERE SEEMS TO BE ANOTHER GUEST ARRIVING.

CAN I HELP YOU, SIR?

UH...YEAH. HI YA THERE, JEEVES. WE WAS JUST WONDERIN' IF WE COULD BORROW A CUP OF SUGAR.

I'M SORRY, THE MAN OF THE HOUSE, MR. RITZFIELD, IS RECENTLY DECEASED. YOU'VE COME AT A VERY AWKWARD TIME.

YEAH, WELL IF HE'S DECEASED 'N' ALL, THEN HE WON'T BE NEEDIN' NO SUGAR, WILL HE?

TOUCHÉ, SIR. WELL PLAYED. I SHALL FETCH YOU A CUP. WON'T YOU COME IN?

SUCK! SUCK!

YOU SEE I HAVE A PROSTHETIC LEG. IF I ATTEMPTED TO PUSH ANYONE, THE FORCE OF MY OWN PUSH WOULD KNOCK ME TO THE FLOOR.

THAT DON'T MEAN YA COULDN'T HAVE DONE IT ANYWAY!

:SIGH: THAT'S TRUE, SIR. EXCEPT FOR THE FACT, YOU MIGHT REMEMBER, THAT I WAS STILL IN THE KITCHEN WHEN THE LIGHTS WENT OUT. I COULD HARDLY RUN IN AND GET BACK OUT IN THAT SHORT OF TIME.

BOY, THIS IS A REAL MIND TICKLER THERE, ANGEL. NO ONE SEEMS TO GOT NO MOTIVE.

ACTUALLY, I NEVER LIKED GIL. I ONCE THREATENED TO PUSH HIM DOWN THE STAIRS IN PUBLIC. I JUST CANNOT STAND THE MAN!

OH, I'M SORRY. YOU WANNA PLAY WITH YOUR LITTLE FRIEND. AW, THAT'S CUTE.

SUCK! SUCK!

BABY'S FIRST SKELETON

I THINK I GOT THIS MYSTERY ALL WRAPPED UP...

SUCK! SUCK! SUCK! SUCK!

...I'M GOIN' WITH MY FIRST CHOICE, THE SISSY! I SAY WE BEAT A CONFESSION OUT OF HIM!

SURELY THERE MUST BE ANOTHER WAY.

AAAH! NO! PLEASE! I-I-I'LL CONFESS TO WHATEVER YOU WANT!

MAYBE WE SHOULD SEE WHERE THIS IS GOING...

SUCK! SUCK!

SNATCH!

WHOA! I'M TRIPPIN' HERE!

OH! MY SPINE!

BONK!

GEEZ, I ALMOST FELL DOWN THEM STAIRS, JUST LIKE--

GASP! I GET IT NOW!

GA-GA-GOO! HEE-HEE!

"GIL DIDN'T GET PUSHED DOWN NO STAIRS! HE MUST'VE PANICKED IN THE DARK!"

I, JONATHAN RITZFIELD III, BEING OF SOUND BODY AND MIND, DO HEREBY--

AH! GOSH DARN IT. MUST'VE BLOWN A FUSE.

"THEN, WE HE WENT TO TURN ON THE LIGHTS, HE TRIPPED, AND FELL DOWN THOSE STAIRS! IT WEREN'T NO MURDER! IT WAS AN *ACCIDENT!*"

DON'T WORRY, OL' GIL WILL--

AAAH!

ACTUALLY, OL' GIL ISN'T EVEN DEAD, AND I WAS LYING RIGHT ON TOP OF THE WILL. HOW DO YA LIKE THAT? THINGS ARE FINALLY LOOKIN' UP!

HE'S A ZOMBIE! KILL HIS BRAIN!

IT'S MY MEDICAL OPINION THAT THIS MAN IS NO ZOMBIE.

OH WELL, MYSTERY SOLVED THEN. WE'D BETTER BE GETTIN' BACK. I GOTTA FEED MAGGIE AND FINISH PEEKIN' INTO THE MEDICINE CABINETS.

OF COURSE, SIR. HERE'S YOUR SUGAR AND THANK YOU FOR "SOLVING" THE MYSTERY.

SUCH THAT IT WAS.

LATER THAT DAY...

OW! QUIT IT. OW! QUIT IT!

WE'RE HOME! WHERE'S MY LITTLE MAGGIE?

AND WHERE'S MY LITTLE MOE?

THE END